Anonymous

A Letter to the Right Honorable Charles James Fox

Anonymous

A Letter to the Right Honorable Charles James Fox

ISBN/EAN: 9783744689229

Printed in Europe, USA, Canada, Australia, Japan

Cover: Foto ©Thomas Meinert / pixelio.de

More available books at **www.hansebooks.com**

A

L E T T E R

TO THE

RIGHT HONORABLE

CHARLES JAMES FOX,

On the late DEBATES upon the DECLARATORY BILL in PARLIAMENT, and in LEADENHALL-STREET.

BY AN INDIA PROPRIETOR.

LONDON:

PRINTED FOR JOHN STOCKDALE, OPPOSITE BURLINGTON-HOUSE, PICCADILLY.

M.DCC.LXXXVIII.

[Price One Shilling and Six-pence.]

A LETTER, &c.

SIR,

YOU have long been repreſented as the champion of liberty in England.—In the opinion of your friends you were ſacrificed a few years ago, becauſe you nobly refuſed to conſent to a diminution of that power, which we the people of England poſſeſs in this happy conſtitution.—Government however had for ſome time been carried on, notwithſtanding your oppoſition, with a remarkable degree of unanimity; and even Mr. Fox, who cannot be ſuppoſed to entertain very favourable ſentiments for the miniſter, ſpoke of his conduct at the commencement

mencement of the present session in terms of great approbation. The prospect has been suddenly clouded, and I am free to confess, that Mr. Pitt's popularity has lately received a blow, from which it will not immediately recover.

I FEEL, I profess, a very strong inclination to state to the public the true grounds of the late warmly-contested disputes in Parliament, and in Leadenhall-street; but before I proceed I must implore your pardon, if unintentionally one libellous expression should escape my pen. I had long conceived, indeed, that such a request to Mr. Fox, of all men living, would have been unnecessary;—but after what has lately happened you will pardon me for making it; and you will, I hope, receive it with indulgence.

IT was impossible, on an Indian question, to avoid a very full discussion of your celebrated Bill; but it is with some surprise I have heard it asserted out of doors, that what has recently happened is a full justification of that bill, and that your friends will go down to the next election with it in their hands,

hands, as their beſt recommendation. From whence could ſuch a deluſion ariſe? If I can truſt my own ears, a majority of thoſe gentlemen who divided with you, did ſo upon terms which, though they do them infinite honour, can afford very little cauſe of triumph to the avowed friends of Mr. Fox:—They left Mr. Pitt becauſe they conceived that he was attempting to obtain a part of that patronage by ſap, the whole of which Mr. Fox would have taken by ſtorm.

PERMIT me very ſhortly to explain what you would have taken, and what Mr. Pitt has legally obtained.

SINCERITY is amongſt the firſt of virtues that a ſtateſman can poſſeſs, perhaps it is the firſt.—You are the only ſtateſman I ever knew or read of, who are ſuppoſed really to poſſeſs ſincerity. I will therefore give you every credit which you can claim, for having fairly avowed in the month of November, 1783, that you would ſeize all the patronage of the Eaſt India Company, both at home and abroad. I give you credit for ſlighting the advice of your friend Mr. Sheridan. You were right not to expunge that offenſive clauſe. Money, ſecurities for money, goods, houſes, warehouſes, down to locks and keys, were meant to be taken, and it was fair in you to ſtate your meaning as roundly as poſſible. May I not without offence, however, preſume, that you placed very great dependance upon a decided and powerful majority in Parliament? You were bold when in your own opinion there was no danger. The Eaſt India Company, ever an object of jealouſy in this country, and very juſtly ſo I freely allow, was peculiarly ſo at the moment you brought in your Bill. She was deſcribed as bankrupt, and not as bankrupt by the calamities of a war, in which the politics of Great-Britain had involved her; but her diſtreſſes were ſuppoſed to ariſe from groſs miſmanagement abroad, and from corrupt connivance at home.—Such was the advantage with which you began the attack. Let me now review very ſhortly the forces which you brought into the field to ſupport you in that attack.

Early in the year 1783, you forced from his Majeſty's councils the Marquis of Lanſ-downe,

downe, and the Lord Chancellor.—True it is, you had not ſtrength to effect this by your own adherents; you therefore called to your aſſiſtance a man, whoſe misfortunes I lament, and whoſe private virtues I revere. That noble Lord, a hoſt in himſelf, had many friends who looked up to him with gratitude for favours received: he had alſo many more friends of another deſcription, who looked up to him for future favours. The gentlemen of both theſe deſcriptions re-echoed with vehemence, the godlike ſentiment you uttered,

"*Inimicitiæ placabiles amicitiæ ſempiterne.*"

Lord Lanſdowne could not withſtand ſuch a combination. He ſaved England by a peace, and, as a reward for ſo great a ſervice, he was permitted to retire unmoleſted to his woods. Of your own adherents, Sir, I ſhall ſay but little: amongſt them are to be found men of extenſive property, not eminent for ſuperior talents; and men of no property, whoſe companionable qualities endear them to all who know them. Theſe deſcriptions of perſons compoſed a large majority in the late

late Houſe of Commons, on whom you could depend, as long as his Majeſty continued you in office.

When your ſcheme was opened, the country took the alarm: but thoſe who had had a nearer opportunity of examining the conduct of miniſters, trembled for the conſtitution. It was aſſerted on the one hand, and not contradicted on the other, that your bill aſſumed all the patronage and all the commerce of the Company in every part of the world. The only ſecurity we had againſt an abuſe of ſuch vaſt powers, was in the irreproachable characters of your commiſſioners; a majority of them were left to you as a legacy by the late Marquis of Rockingham. Earl Fitzwilliam was his nephew and his heir; Mr. Montague, Mr. Gregory, and Sir Henry Fletcher, were ſtrenuous members of that party. Let me therefore, Sir, ſtating what the Marquis did, aſſume for a moment, that they would have followed his example. One great ſecurity againſt corrupt patronage in India is, that the officer and the civil ſervice riſe by ſeniority; and though abuſes may prevail, and doubtleſs have prevailed, even where this rule is obſerved, ſtill it is the beſt poſſible ſecurity that can be deviſed againſt the corrupt exerciſe of patronage. But ſo far was the Marquis of Rockingham and his friends above the pain of beſtowing a moment's attention upon the juſt rights of the Company's ſervants, that in one day, in the year 1782, nine young majors were promoted to the rank of lieutenant-colonels in India only, and nine young lieutenant-colonels to the rank of colonels in India only; thereby effectually precluding the old officers of the Company from every poſſibility of command and diſtinction in their own ſervice.

In the ſame year, 1782, the Marquis of Rockingham, at the requiſition of Mr. Burke, agreed to the appointment of his couſin William Burke to the office of pay-maſter of the king's forces in India. This was, in fact, the creation of a new and uſeleſs office; and it was beſtowed upon a man who had ſtolen out to India againſt law; who at the time was the avowed agent of an Indian Rajah, and was abſolutely incapacitated for fifteen months after he received the nation's money,

 from

from executing any ſervice in return, ſuppoſing there had been any thing for him to do.

Sir Henry Fletcher, for the purpoſes of patronage, and patronage only, overloaded all the eſtabliſhments of the Company in India, civil and military, when the war was actually at an end. The conſequence is, that ſince 1783 to this day, neither a writer nor a cadet has been appointed.

Now, Mr. Fox, may I not fairly preſume, from theſe inſtances, that when the whole civil and military patronage of India was thrown into the hands of that party which had abuſed, as far as they could abuſe, the powers formerly entruſted to them, may I not ſuppoſe, I ſay, that with India at their feet, they would have uſed it for the purpoſes of their own ambition and future ſecurity? The concluſion is evident.

Without entering into any invidious examination of the characters of thoſe who compoſed what is called the Coalition Adminiſtration, I may fairly ſay, that they were

in

in general men of deſperate fortunes. I do not mean the Cabinet, though even there I could point out ſome who with great landed property were univerſally known to have been involved in pecuniary difficulties; but I mean principally the ſecond and third ranks, the efficient men of that adminiſtration. Of theſe there were many of family, without fortune; and many without either family or fortune. To ſuch men, conceive for a moment what a mine was opened. A thouſand guineas was publicly offered for a writer's appointment: and if, according to Mr. Burgoyne's expreſſion on a former occaſion, the Company's ſervice was rotten to the core, would you have been at a loſs for arguments to juſtify a general removal? Why, Sir, the incumbrances in Drury-lane and the Hay-market, and the mortgage upon a Buckinghamſhire freehold, might have been cleared in a fortnight. In a word, Mr. Fox, your bill veſted ſuch powers of patronage in ſeven men, as cannot be veſted in any men without ruin to this conſtitution; and the men in whom you did veſt the power, were as likely, from the circumſtances which I have mentioned, to abuſe that power, as any ſeven men in England.

BEFORE your bill had gone through two branches of the legiſlature, it was perfectly underſtood: we heard, it is true, a great deal of nonſenſe about back ſtairs, and ſecret influence; but the fact is now generally acknowledged, that the Marquis of Buckingham demanded an audience of his Majeſty, and openly, avowedly, and unequivocally, gave his ſentiments of the bill to the Sovereign. It is generally acknowledged, that in ſo doing the noble Marquis acted conſtitutionally; and as to any means afterwards uſed to obtain a majority againſt your bill, I fancy the activity on the one part could not exceed the induſtry on the other.

I NOW come to Mr. PITT's adminiſtration.—On its firſt formation, you predicted its duration not to exceed Twelfth Day; but the deluſion, as you termed it, has been of long continuance.

IN the month of Auguſt, 1784, Mr. Pitt's bill was paſſed. This bill left to the Eaſt-India

India Company the entire management of its commerce. It left to the Company all appointments to offices, both at home and abroad. The minister refused what the Company had agreed to concede to him, the power of appointing governors, and commanders in chief. The bill vested in a Board, to be nominated by his Majesty, the controul and direction of all powers, civil, military, and financial, in India.

I PROTEST to you, Sir, that I do not conceive the imagination of man could frame a system more perfect, attending at the same time to that just jealousy as to the patronage of India, which has marked this, and I trust will mark every future House of Commons.

LET us, Mr. Fox, examine what effects this bill has produced. It passed in the month of August 1784. In the March preceding, the sword was completely sheathed in India. In that month, a peace was concluded with the last, and the most formidable of our enemies, Tippoo Sultaun; and we had the satisfaction to reflect, that through an arduous ſtruggle, againſt an hoſt of foes, India had been preſerved to Great-Britain.

At one and the ſame moment, œconomical retrenchments were forming in Great-Britain, and carrying into effect in India; and although I am willing to allow the Board of Controul the merit of great attention to the affairs of the Eaſt-India Company, yet I utterly deny them that merit which their partiſans have aſſumed for them, I mean the merit of ſaving to the Company a million and a half ſterling in their annual expenditure in India. They have the merit of approving what was done in India by the Company's ſervants, and in Great-Britain by the Court of Directors, and no more.

It cannot be denied, but that the King's miniſter, or the commiſſioners, for they are in fact the ſame, poſſeſſed that influence in the direction which miniſters ever have poſſeſſed. In fact, the King's miniſter has almoſt invariably appointed to the high ſituations in India. Mr. Haſtings was four ſeveral times appointed governor-general of Bengal, by the legiſlature, on the recommendation

tion of Lord North. Mr. Wheler, Mr. Stables, and Sir John Macpherſon, were appointed members of the ſupreme council, on the recommendation, or through the influence of Lord North. The ſame influence placed Sir Eyre Coote at the head of the army, and ſent Sir Thomas Rumbold, and Sir Hector Munro to Madras: and it was once a very ſtrong complaint which you, Mr. Fox, made againſt your friend Lord Sandwich, that he had acquired ſuch a corrupt influence in the Eaſt-India Company, that he was enabled to counteract every effort which you made to remove him from the Admiralty.

I AFFIRM, that miniſterial influence at the India-houſe has been leſs ſince Mr. Pitt's bill paſſed, than at any former period. General Sloper was appointed to Bengal, and Sir John Dalling to Madras, without any recommendation from the miniſter, and I believe in direct oppoſition to his wiſhes. The ſubſequent appointments of Earl Cornwallis, Sir Archibald Campbell, and General Meadows, were in fact Mr. Pitt's appointments, in the ſame manner that Mr. Wheler's, Mr.

Stables',

Stables', and Sir John Macpherſon's, were Lord North's. But is there no difference between allowing the Miniſter to retain that ſpecies of influence at the India-houſe, which a miniſter always has had, and throwing the entire patronage, both in India and in Great-Britain, into the hands of ſeven commiſſioners?

The tranquillity that reigns in the Carnatic, the increaſe of population and of cultivation, the extinction of parties, and the ſatisfaction ſo ſtrongly expreſſed by the old Nabob, are proofs that the deciſion as to his debts was a wiſe one. That many bonds were granted by the old man, not for money received, I believe; but unleſs he will himſelf diſcriminate thoſe from the reſt, which he is earneſtly deſired to do, I ſee not the poſſibility of diſcovering by any other means what bonds were *bona fide* granted for money received, and what were gratuitouſly given by the Nabob, to their original holders.

The next important act in the adminiſtration of India, was that moſt ſalutary law, by which the powers of the revenues in India were

were confiderably enlarged. The beneficial effects of this fyftem we now experience. Great power, and great refponfibility are now lodged where they ought to remain. The patronage of India, is where only it can be fafely placed, in India; and the legiflature has guarded, as far as human wifdom can guard, againft even an improper exercife of patronage in India.—Offices and falaries are claffed—attention to feniority is ftrictly enjoined—nor have I heard a fingle inftance of partiality in the difpofal of offices attributed to Earl Cornwallis fince his acceffion to the government.

I COME now to that fubject which has occafioned the late difcuffions in both Houfes of Parliament, and in Leadenhall-ftreet.

AFTER Sir Archibald Campbell was appointed Governor of Madras, he was employed to form the feveral military eftablifhments in India. Thefe were fubmitted to the Court of Directors, and are printed by order of the Houfe of Commons. Some Gentlemen in the Direction, whofe ideas differed from thofe of General Campbell, propofed that the plans ſhould be ſubmitted to Mr. Haſtings, who had lately returned from Bengal.—His remarks are alſo printed: and his opinions coinciding with thoſe of the Directors, it was determined to add one third to the number of Europeans in Bengal, more than thoſe which Mr. Campbell had propoſed. The Board of Controul demurred at firſt, but afterwards adopted the alterations; and the eſtabliſhment of Bengal was fixed at about five thouſand Europeans, and thirty-ſix battalions of Sepoys.

GENERAL CAMPBELL's eſtabliſhment for Bombay, was far beyond the ability of that unproductive iſland to ſupport; and for Madras, it was ſo large as to abſorb the whole of its revenues. Fortunately it is ſtill an eſtabliſhment upon paper only, and upon paper only I hope it will remain.

LAST year, when we fully expected a war, the attention of the King's miniſters was naturally turned to India. Is it criminal in them to endeavour to correct an error as ſoon as they diſcover it? They did diſcover, that the European force in India was too low, for the importance and value of that empire to

Great-

Great-Britain, and for the dangers to which it might eventually be expofed.

Now, Mr. Fox, let me put this plain question to you. The Board of Controul in 1785, fix a military eftablifhment for India, in virtue of the powers vefted in them by law. The Directors think it too fmall at Bengal; they tell the Commiffioners they think fo; the Commiffioners *confent* to increafe the Europeans one-third.

In 1787, the Commiffioners think, with the addition of that third, that it is ftill too fmall a force, and they require a confiderable addition. I afk you then, if they had the power to fix a fmall eftablifhment in 1785, had they not alfo the power to fix a larger in 1787, if upon better information, or from a more perfect knowledge of the fubject, they were enabled to correct their former errors?

In fact, the true queftion is, *not* whether they had the power, but whether they exercifed *that power* properly; whether they did, or did not facrifice the interefts of the Eaft-India Company, in adding fo many more kin[illegible] officers to their eſtabliſhment; and whether ſuch additions were made from a patriotic attention to the public ſervice, or from a wiſh to increaſe their own patronage. It is extraordinary that theſe queſtions have never yet been argued. I will therefore aſſume it as a fact, that from ſome documents before you, of which I am ignorant, you were convinced that the Company could not have raiſed eighteen hundred men in the month of October laſt,—and that the great difficulty of the whole is removed, by the arrangement that has taken place, as to the rank of the Company's officers, who, although they are not relieved to the full extent of their petition, have received very great relief indeed; and in one point, full and complete relief.—I mean from that intolerable grievance which was impoſed upon them by that adminiſtration, in which you bore a conſiderable ſhare, in 1782, when brevet local rank was granted to twenty of his Majeſty's field officers.

It was almoſt impoſſible in ſo many ſucceſſive debates on an Indian queſtion, not to allude to a certain great cauſe now depending in Weſtminſter-Hall. In me, however, it would

would be highly indecent to venture a word upon this delicate ſubject; but to a ſimple matter of fact I may ſpeak, and to that fact I am ſure I ſhall have your aſſent.

You have been repreſented as ſtanding forth in the preſent moment as the avenger of the wrongs of oppreſſed millions, and as relieving the miſeries of thoſe, who can only repay you by their prayers to Heaven. This is jargon, this is nonſenſe, Mr. Fox, which you have manlineſs enough to deſpiſe—for you know it is not true, in any one ſenſe of the word. What you would have done, had your Bill paſſed, I cannot preſume to ſay; but what Mr. Pitt has done I know, and I will proceed to ſtate it.—

He has raiſed the ſtock of the Eaſt India Company from one hundred and eighteen to one hundred and ſeventy; but I deny, that in ſo doing, he has no more merit than what is due to him for raiſing the three per cents. from fifty-five to ſeventy-ſix.—For if the preamble of your Bill were true, that diſorders of an alarming nature prevailed in India, and were increaſing, and that the affairs of India would fall into utter ruin, if a fitting a fitting remedy were not inſtantly provided; then to Mr. Pitt is due the credit of providing that fitting remedy. Will you accept this, or will you allow me to ſay that your preamble was falſe?—One or the other I muſt ſay.

The real fact would be moſt unqueſtionably, that had your preamble been true, the merits of Mr. Pitt and Mr. Dundas are beyond all praiſe. It could not be diſputed, that they have found that "fit and becoming "remedy," which has prevented our affairs from falling "into utter ruin;" and they would have the additional merit of having done all this, without giving the conſtitution ſuch a wound as it could never have ſurvived. Better India be loſt, than that the liberties of Engliſhmen be overturned.

We are now advanced to that particular ſtage of Indian enquiries, which mocks all oratory.—A pathetic ſpeech may be made—a lady may faint—the moſt exquiſite ſorrow may be affected, when the imaginary ſufferings of millions are deſcribed, by thoſe who deſpiſe both the laws of God and man; who can ſee the diſtreſſes of hundreds unmoved; who,

who, in many inſtances, may occaſion thoſe diſtreſſes, by contracting debts which they have not the moſt diſtant proſpect of paying. Yet, Mr. Fox, the public judgment muſt be governed hereafter by their opinion of facts, which ſhall be proved beyond the power of contradiction. Let me try your preamble by this teſt, and I challenge the whole world to contradict any one aſſertion that I ſhall make.

On the 18th of November, 1783, your preamble ſtated, " that diſorders of an " alarming nature and magnitude had long " prevailed, and do ſtill continue and in- " creaſe; and that the affairs of the Com- " pany would probably fall into utter ruin, " if an immediate and fitting remedy were " not provided."

That no immediate and fitting remedy has been provided to this day, you have conſtantly aſſerted. Let me therefore ſtate how we have exiſted in India without it. At the moment you brought in your Bill, hoſtilities had ceaſed in every part of Indoſtan; and peace upon terms ſecure, honourable, and advantageous,

advantageous, had been concluded with every European and native power in India, except Tippoo Sultaun. With him a negociation had commenced, and the peace was ſigned in the month of March following.

In Bengal and its dependencies, we enjoyed, at the time your Bill was brought in, the moſt perfect tranquility—the natives were then, as they are now, "the happieſt, "and beſt protected ſubjects in India." Our Treaſury was indeed low; but that was the natural conſequence of having ſent ſix millions ſterling to Madras and Bombay, during the late arduous war. What Mr. Haſtings predicted very ſoon after your Bill was before the Houſe of Commons, has in fact happened. He ventured to aſſure the Court of Directors, in the month of December, 1783, that a very few years of peace would effectually relieve Bengal from all its incumbrances.—Of the ſtate of Madras I ſhall ſay but little. Your opinion of the relative rights of the Nabob of Arcot, and the Rajah of Tanjore, you have naturally imbibed from Mr. Burke. His ſentiments reſpecting them are very well known; and a clauſe in his

Subsidiary Bill was admirably calculated to prevent that tranquility which now happily reigns upon the coast of Coromandel. Bombay was in 1783, a dead load upon us.—It is so still; and it is beyond the ingenuity of either Mr. Fox or Mr. Pitt, to make it otherwise. I affirm, therefore, with confidence, that though you asserted India to be in a dangerous state, you totally failed in your proof; and though you predicted utter ruin if your Bill did not pass, yet the actual state of India now, and for some years past, most fully refutes your assertion.

In the arduous struggle for power, which followed the rejection of your Bill, India was totally forgotten—But did any bad consequence follow? At length Mr. Pitt became firmly established in his office. He met this Parliament with a new India Bill, and it passed into a law in August, 1784.

During the progress of both bills through the House of Commons, we heard several admirable dissertations upon government; and I, for one, fully subscribe to your excellent doctrine, that all governments are, or ought to be, eſtabliſhed for the happineſs of the governed. But in contradiction to this excellent principle, the Britiſh government in India is moſt unqueſtionably eſtabliſhed for the benefit of Great-Britain. In all the ſucceſſions of miniſters and directors, from our firſt acquiſition of Bengal to the preſent moment, however humane we may be in theory, I have obſerved, that every miniſter has ſhewn a laudable zeal to turn to the beſt advantage for the public, the vaſt revenues which we enjoy in Indoſtan.

WHAT your ſeven directors would have done, I will not pretend to ſay; but what the preſent Board of Controul have done, I know; and I think you will agree with me, that the following ſtate of their tranſactions is ſtrictly conſonant to truth.

WE were told by Mr. Burke, that in the year 1772, the government of Bengal expoſed all the nobility and country gentlemen of a great kingdom to ſale. This was deſcribed as one of the moſt wicked and wanton acts of tyranny and arbitrary power ever practiſed in any country; and ſo undoubtedly

edly it would have been, were the fact really so.

You are now, Sir, sufficiently versed in oriental learning, to know, that in Indostan the lands are the property of the sovereign. You must know also, that a zemindar is an officer of government appointed to collect the rents on the part of government. You must have heard also, that the directors at home, and many of our best-informed countrymen in India, actually believed in the year 1772, that Mahomed Reza Cawn had defrauded the Company of many millions sterling, and that the only possible mode by which the Company could attain a knowledge of the actual value of the lands, was by letting them to the highest bidder. It was in vain however to represent a word upon this subject while you were in the plenitude of your power. Mr. Burke, who was never in India, and Mr. Francis, who, though six years there, never could speak a syllable to a Zemindar in his own language, (and a Zemindar knows no other) these gentlemen, I say, had formed an ingenious system, from which it would have been treachery to depart.

With these strong ideas of the rights of Zemindars, the present Board of Controul succeeded to the superintendance and direction of the revenues of Bengal. But mark, I pray you, the difference between theory and practice;—they have ordered that system to be adopted, the wisdom of which was never disputed, and which in fact has been precisely the system pursued since the English have managed the revenues of Bengal; that is, that in all practicable instances the lands shall be let to Zemindars. In Bengal there are four very large zemindaries, Burdwan, Dinagapore, Rajeshay, and Nuddea. In the two first, the zemindars are minors, the third belongs to a woman, and the fourth only can be managed by the zemindar himself.

In these, as in all the zemindaries, the amount of the settlement, or rent, is fixed by government; the zemindar has the first option, but if he refuses to take it, either the collection is made Rhass, that is, government by its own officers collects the rents, or it is let to a farmer. At the present moment, almost the whole province of Bahar is let to farmers, by a settlement formed by Mr.

Mr. Shore; and above one half of the province of Bengal is let to farmers. The late consultations are filled with instances of the dispossession of zemindars, and the sale of their property, to make good their arrears of rent to government; and almost the last revenue act which we have received from Bengal, sanctioned by Lord Cornwallis, was the sale of a part of the zemindary of the Rannee of Rajeshay, because she had fallen in arrears in her rents.

WHEN therefore Mr. Dundas asserted, that the Board of Controul had given security to the landholders in Bengal, I was much pleased to hear you call out for the proofs of that assertion. The landholders have, in fact, the same security for that species of property which they hold in the land, that they have had at any one time. One very beneficial regulation they have indeed ordered to be enforced, but that regulation has been repeatedly recommended from Bengal; it is this, that the lands should be let at fixed rents, upon very long leases. They have the merit also of resisting the ingenious reasonings of a speculative man, Mr. James Grant,

Grant, who has confidently asserted, that the zemindar's of Bengal have defrauded government of a very large sum annually; and they have the merit also (if my information on this point be true) of declaring that they will give the zemindars of Bengal certain rights in the soil, which the government of Bengal have lately declared they do not possess.

From this short account it will appear clearly evident, that the Board of Controul have made no alteration in the revenue system, except that which was recommended some years ago from Bengal.

If you examine our foreign system, you will find it precisely the same that it has been for some years past. No proposition has been made for the restoration of Cheyt Sing. On the contrary, the government of Bengal has, by the last dispatch, assured the Directors, that the province of Benares is in a most flourishing state, and that the revenues will be fully realized. The Directors and the Board of Controul in reply, have expressed their great satisfaction at this intelligence,

gence, and desire every attention may be used, to preserve the interest which the Company has in that valuable zemindary.

LET us pass on to Oude, and the extensive dominions of the Nabob Vizier; you will find that the system established the 31st of December, 1783, has been rigidly adhered to. We have received all arrears from the Nabob; we protect his dominions from foreign invasion, and he pays us for the forces employed for this purpose, and all incidental expences, fifty lacks of sicca rupees.

HYDER BEG KHAN, of whom we have heard so much, is still his minister, and was received by Earl Cornwallis with every possible mark of attention and regard.

AFTER this short detail, allow me to affirm, Mr. Fox, that Bengal was at no time in danger of falling into utter ruin; that the temporary distresses to which it was subject were occasioned by the politics of Great-Britain; and that by its own vigour and exertions it had actually relieved itself from those diſtreſſes, at the very moment when you perſuaded the people of England, that India was ruined, and when you ſunk the ſtock in one day from one hundred and thirty-five to one hundred and eighteen.

A FEW words before I conclude upon the difference between the two celebrated Bills.—We have the experience of four years that India can be preſerved, and that it can flouriſh under the ſyſtem eſtabliſhed by Mr. Pitt's Bill.—We have the experience of two years, that the extraordinary powers granted to Earl Cornwallis and Sir Archibald Campbell, are in the higheſt degree beneficial. Yet Mr. Burke told us, when they were granted, that they went to eſtabliſh deſpotiſm and arbitrary power. I have ſince been aſked by fifty people, "Don't you "think what Burke ſaid about arbitrary "power in Weſtminſter-Hall, was vaſtly "fine?" Yet, though I abhor the idea of arbitrary power in Great-Britain, I know that our governments in India ever have poſſeſſed, and ever muſt poſſeſs it: and I am better pleaſed that it ſhould reſt as it does

now,

now, in a governor, than in the majority of a council.

The ſyſtem then, as perfected by Mr. Pitt, for the government of India, is this, that our governors, taking the reſponſibility upon themſelves, ſhould have the power of acting according to the dictates of their own judgment in all caſes of difficulty.

That in the diſpoſal of offices in India, ſeniority ſhould be attended to as ſtrictly as poſſible; but that at all events the patronage of India, ſhould be diſpoſed of in India.

That the patronage to be given away in England, ſhould all be at the diſpoſal of the Court of Directors. By them all contracts for exports are made—all offices at the India-Houſe are filled—all ſhips are appointed to voyages—and when Sir Henry Fletcher's ſupernumeraries no longer exiſt, by the Directors will all cadets and writers be appointed. Poſſibly a member of the Board of Controul may be able to get a good Bengal voyage. I know we have a Henry Dundas, and a Melville Caſtle, a Pitt, and

 a Wila William Pitt, a Lord Mulgrave, and a Lord Walſingham, amongſt our ſhips; but it can only be by procuring the nomination of one of the Directors—an influence which Lord North, and every other miniſter enjoyed in the ſame manner.

By your bill there was no check of any kind eſtabliſhed. Your commiſſioners had the entire removal of every perſon in office, either at home or abroad. They had the power of making as many new appointments, or creating as many new offices, as they ſhould think proper. They were ſubject to no controul. The proprietors had the permiſſion to aſſemble once in three months, to hear their accounts read to them. The natural conſequence of this great change would have been, that the patronage of India, and of Great-Britain as connected with India, was gone from Leadenhall-ſtreet for ever. I have not only my dividend to receive upon the preſent ſyſtem, but I may look forward to the appointment of a ſon or a nephew to India hereafter, through my connections in Leadenhall-ſtreet. Many other proprietors have the ſame proſpects. But could we have

gone

gone to Brooks's, to Drury-lane, or to Beaconsfield? Yet we muſt have gone there to ſolicit for appointments, had your Bill paſſed into a law.

EVERY man who has the welfare of his country at heart, muſt ſincerely rejoice that the late ample diſcuſſions have taken place in Parliament. The country Gentlemen were alarmed, perhaps more than the occaſion warranted; yet if there was an error, it was on the ſafe ſide. It proves to me, that the Company's Charter muſt be renewed; nor can the imagination of man conceive any poſſible mode by which India can be retained under the dominion of Great-Britain, unleſs through the medium of a company, without danger to our liberties.

COLONEL BARRE deſcribed very juſtly, and with great accuracy, the various channels into which the patronage at preſent ran. The miniſter has called upon us to watch him and his colleagues; and there never will be wanting in this or in any future Houſe of Commons, men who will have ſagacity

to

to deteſt every attempt that ſhall be made by the Board of Controul, to encroach upon that patronage, which the law has placed in the hands of the Eaſt-India Company.

I am, SIR,

Your moſt obedient

humble Servant,

March 25, 1788.

A PROPRIETOR *of India Stock.*

N E W B O O K S,

Printed for John Stockdale.

1. SERMONS on IMPORTANT and INTERESTING SUBJECTS. By the Rev. Percival Stockdale. Price 6s.

2. HISTORY of VIRGINIA. By his Excellency Thomas Jefferson. In One Volume, 8vo. Price 7s.

3. History of NEW HOLLAND; with an Introductory Discourse on Banishment. By the Right Hon. William Eden. In One Volume, 8vo. Price [illegible]

4. HISTORY of the REVOLUTION of SOUTH CAROLINA. By Dr. David Ramsay. In Two Volumes, 8vo. Price 12s.

5. HISTORY of the UNION. By Daniel De Foe. With an Introduction, by J. L. De Lolme. In One large Quarto Volnme, containing 1000 Pages. Price 1l. 10s.

6. HISTORICAL TRACTS. By Sir John Davies. In One Volume, 8vo. Price 5s.

7. DEBATES in PARLIAMENT. By Dr. Samuel Johnson. In Two Volumes, 8vo. Price 12s.

8. SHAKSPEARE's PLAYS. Complete in One Volume, 8vo. Price 15s.

9. ORIGI-

9. ORIGINAL ROYAL LETTERS, written by King Charles the Ist and IId, King James the IId, the King and Queen of Bohemia, &c. In One Volume, with Four elegant Engravings by Sherwin. Price 10s. 6d.

10. POEMS on various Subjects. By Henry James Pye, Esq; M. P. In Two Volumes, 8vo. Price 12s.

11. FOUR TRACTS. By Thomas Day, Esq; In One Volume, 8vo. Price 9s.

12. BEAUTIES of the BRITISH SENATE. In Two Volumes, 8vo. Price 10s. 6d.

13. An ESTIMATE of the COMPARATIVE STRENGTH of GREAT-BRITAIN, during the present and four preceding Reigns, and of the LOSSES of her TRADE from every WAR since the REVOLUTION. By George Chalmers, Esq; Price 3s. 6d. sewed, or 5s. bound in Calf, and lettered.

14. A BRIEF ESSAY on the ADVANTAGES and DISADVANTAGES which respectively attend FRANCE and GREAT-BRITAIN with regard to TRADE. By Josiah Tucker, D. D. Dean of Gloucester. Price 2s.

15. The CHILDREN's MISCELLANY,

> Bid him, besides, his daily Pains employ
> To form the tender Manners of the Boy;
> And work him, like a waxen Babe, with Art,
> To perfect Symmetry in every Part. DRYDEN.

Ornamented with a beautiful Frontispiece. Price 3s. in Boards, or 3s. 6d. bound.

NEW

NEW PUBLICATIONS
For the EAST-INDIES,

Printed for John Stockdale.

1. THE TRIBUNAL, addressed to the Peers of Great-Britain, sitting in Judgment on Warren Hastings. Price 2s. 6d.

2. The INDIAN VOCABULARY; to which is prefixed, the Forms of Impeachments. 3s. 6d.

3. Mr. BURKE's CHARGES, and Mr. HASTINGS's DEFENCE. In One large Volume, 8vo. Price 10s. 6d.

4. MINUTES of the EVIDENCE, complete. In One Volume, 8vo. Price 7s. 6d.

5. ARTICLES of IMPEACHMENT against WARREN HASTINGS, Esq; Price 2s. 6d.

6. The ANSWER of WARREN HASTINGS, Esq; to the above Articles. Price 4s.

7. A NARRATIVE of the INSURRECTION at BENARES. By Warren Hastings, Esq.

8. The PRESENT STATE of the EAST-INDIES. By Warren Hastings, Esq. Price 2s.

9. MINUTES of WARREN HASTINGS and P. FRANCIS, Esqrs. relative to their Personal Quarrel. Price 1s. 6d.

10. The SPEECH of R. B. SHERIDAN, Esq; on the Charge against Warren Hastings, Esq. 3s.

NEW PUBLICATIONS.

11. The DEBATE on the ROHILLA WAR. 1s. 6d.

12. The DEBATE on Mr. HASTINGS's Conduct to CHEYT SING, at Benares, Price 1s.

13. The DEBATE on the EAST-INDIA RELIEF BILL, Price 1s.

14. REMARKS on Colonel Fullarton's View of the English Interest in India, Price 1s. 6d.

15. REFLEXIONS on Impeaching and Impeachments, Price 1s.

16. The IMPEACHMENT, a Mock Heroic Poem, Price 1s. 6d.

17. A LETTER from the Committee of the House of Commons, to P. Francis, Esq. with REMARKS, 1s.

18. MEMOIRS of the MOGUL EMPIRE. By Captain Jonathan Scott. Price 4s.

19. The BENGAL CALENDAR, for 1788. Price 1s. 6d.

20. Sir GILBERT ELLIOT's CHARGES against Sir ELIJAH IMPEY. Price 2s. 6d.

21. The DEBATES of the LORDS and COMMONS of the LAST SESSION. In Three Vols. 8vo. Price 1l. 1s. half-bound and lettered.

☞ The above DEBATES contain a full Account of the Proceedings respecting Mr. HASTINGS, and the East-India Affairs.

UC SOUTHERN REGIONAL LIBRARY FACILITY
A 000 017 749 3

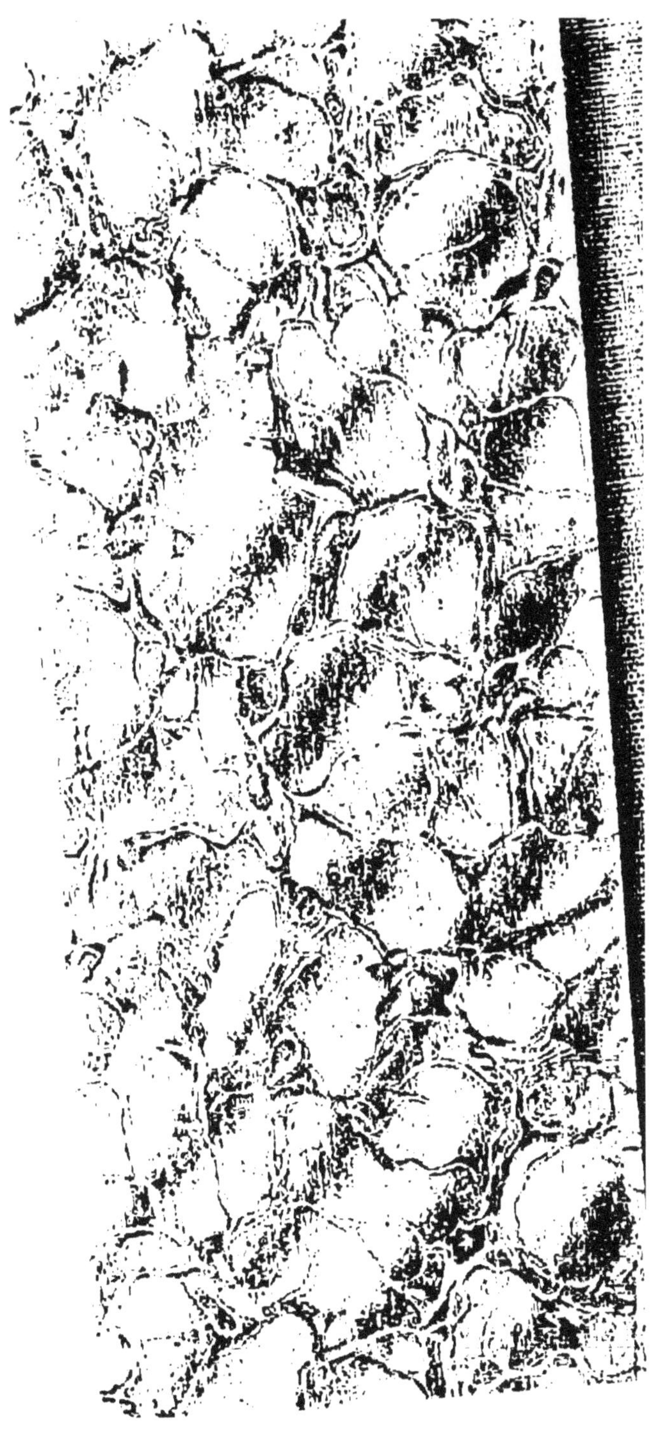

www.ingramcontent.com/pod-product-compliance
Lightning Source LLC
Chambersburg PA
CBHW021429090426
42739CB00009B/1407

* 9 7 8 3 7 4 4 6 8 9 2 2 9 *